Eros Dancing My Soul

Maria Psanis

authorHOUSE®

AuthorHouse™
1663 Liberty Drive
Bloomington, IN 47403
www.authorhouse.com
Phone: 1 (800) 839-8640

Cover Designed by Maria Psanis

Published by AuthorHouse 01/02/2018

ISBN: 978-1-5462-2038-1 (sc)
ISBN: 978-1-5462-2037-4 (hc)
ISBN: 978-1-5462-2097-8 (e)

Library of Congress Control Number: 2017918806

Print information available on the last page.

Th is book is printed on acid-free paper.

Contents

Poetry Books by Maria Psanis

** The Free Inhibited Child (1980)
** Thoughts, Love and You (1981)
** Immortal Shadows (1983)
** Today's Tears, Tomorrow's Laughter (1984)
** Searching for You (1989)
** Breaking the Cycle (1997)
** Asomatos Erotas (Bodiless Love) (2000)
** I Forgot to Ask God (2001)
** Agapi ke Thanatos (Love and Death) (2003)
** a Child, a Dream, and a Sling-shot (2008)
** The Wildflower and the Honey Bee (2011)
** Whispering Kisses Embroidering Love on My Soul (2016)
** Eros Dancing My Soul (2018)

To Maro for stirring my soul . . .
and to Jesus for holding my hand . . .

Letting Go

Letting go of you
is like having to let go
of love, the moon, the stars,
the ocean, the mountains,
the sun, the clouds, the rain,
the music, the song, the dance…

Letting go of you is like
having to let go of life.

Your Name

I speak your name
every time I'm awake,
every time I'm at sleep.
Your name comes to me.
Your darkness dances with
my tears.

My light dances with your wounds.
Echoes the painful love
that binds us together.
Clinging souls
breathing each other's fire.

You move and I move with you.
I separate my heart
and your heart bleeds.
I'm losing me in your senses
as your moon and stars
dive powerless roaring in my flames.

Bigger than God

You come every night
abruptly catching my attention.
In my silence
you become bigger than God,
enlightening my pain.

You tease my dreams,
you mock my passion,
twisting tears and laughter
into suspicious desires.

You drag your soul
upon my sorrowful butterfly
kicking dust and rain,
hurting my autumn wind.

I dare not to reach out,
my garden is wilted,
my wildflowers form
your divine image
as your colorful games
burned me to ashes.

Longing

I have reasons to weep
yet my warrior boldly
forces me to smile.
My labors for dreams
exhaust my thoughts.
Nude in front of my mirror
dreading to see
the wind of my destiny.

Oh sweet-bitter desires
don't throw me in madness,
my heart is blind.
Restless longing for your sea
afraid to dive.

I try to dance,
I try to sing
as I shake off your moonlight.
Nursing drooping hopes
from my sneaky doubts.
Weeping in silence
as darkness plowed my night.

My Silence

A thousand memories
harvest my earth of you.
Clover and honey
touched my dry lips,
my eyes dark brown chocolate
dripping on my cheeks
messing the pink roses from my face.

I normally do not cry.

My silence
the music of my soul
deployed your chattering
in my lost and found sunsets.
Unable to keep your tongue tied.

Reserved, noiseless
tolerant of your intolerance,
your maze I can't walk.
Pushing your darkness,
your avaricious love shallowed
the nectar from my flowers.

Watching

Staring at the sunset
I hear the echoes of your soul,
your eyes hidden behind clouds.
I, stoical,
watching your colors unfolding,
piercing my innocent spring river,
wondering when you're
going to stop your bawling.

Your moonlight crawled
up my spine
vibrating my heart with sea-breeze,
stealing my air and rain.

Staring at the sunset
I see your face covered in silver light.
Your sorrowful noise
captured my empathy
as I grieve the loss
of your sparkling eyes.

You Come and Go

The shadows of your love
marked the growth of my soul.
A thousand songs singing
as my knight failed to
acknowledge the harsh light
stabbing and choking
my heart's delight.
You come and go
with fancy words,
with shameful pain.
Your stormy arrows unattended
rapturing the Eros that
for centuries has swept us
in a ball of sun and moon.

You dance with me in chaos.
You run away from me when holy.
You tease. You hide. You blame.
I walk away. You cry.
My knight in war
with your explosive plight.

Your eyes

My rendezvous with your eyes
was delayed by days, months, years.
I haven't forgotten to give you my hand,
leading you out of your broken winters
and shuttering dark lands.

Time for me has stopped
as I gazed to quench my heart.
Only your eyes I see
over the mountains, oceans, skies.
Only your eyes like magnets
keep me still.
Breathing your thunders,
embracing your woes,
giving you light from my silent soul.

My rendezvous with your eyes
at midnight approach my sleep.
They fill my dreams with anticipation,
visiting me for a short time
before starting my search all over again.
Capturing your glance subsides my hunger.

Your Touch

I love your wildflower skin,
your black hair when tangles with my wind.
Your eyes as they flirt
with my bashful heart,
your touch upon my soul
leaving me
speechless in front of your volcano.

I love the twinkles in your eyes,
your dainty gestures wrapping my silence
with your elegant embrace.
Your trembling love songs in my ears
cause my earth to fall under my waves.

I love the way I stumble on your words.
You say one thing bewildering my pathos,
your exotic melody a dance for my soul,
your voice a lullaby in my precipitous nights.

I love loving you without expectations.
Kissing your air enlightens my sluggish path.

You Reside Inside My Soul

You reside inside my soul.
Your voice dwells in my heart.
I hear your footsteps swinging
and spinning, glowing
my thoughts with your unattainable love.

My grief intertwines with
your tears and pain.
Vigilant, eavesdropping
to hear and feel your radiance,
catching your bright star
with my thirsty lips.

You reside inside my soul.
Your every movement caresses
my naked scars.
Moaning for your eyes to
submerge with my absent minded glance.

You reside inside my soul.

Remedy

Once our eyes touched
I died over and over,
every day, eternity.
Folding your darkness
inch by inch
fearing not to break
your fragile parts.

Your meadow filled with
wildflowers, thorns and nettle,
stifling my walk.

Many times I had to stop.
Wounded me I reached God.
Don't be afraid.
The only remedy I have is love.
I've never been away.
You're the light in my heart.

Willing to Die

I kneeled in front of your soul,
without a mind and body.
A prayer flew out of my fire,
pleasing my exuberant desire.

Moving against the herd,
alone in my desert,
an ocean erupted from my vision,
carrying your broken music as
I kissed your hand that stabbed me
to the ground.

Your cross covered with wounds
I held it pricelessly on my back.
Intimate with your teary eyes
nursing your flooded skies,
falling on my knees. I cried.

I kneeled in front of your soul
willing to die. I wept.
Yearning to dance with your soul
one last time.
Before I die.

Confession

I want to whisper in your ear
but I want no one to hear
my confession.
Come closer, much closer,
don't be afraid.
My voice a river in your blood
will stir up your joyful soul,
your untamed heart,
and make you giggle like a child.
Allow me to kiss
the dew from your eyes,
to touch your face
with my songs.
Don't be afraid.
Come closer, much closer.
Trust without fear.
Have faith in my earthquake
as you observe fireworks
ignited by our Holy unification.
I want to whisper in your ear.
Come closer, much closer.
Did you hear?
You're my echoes
in my trillion galaxies.

Raise You Up

I couldn't step down
to your level.
I had to raise you up
step by step.
All the way up to my heart.

You weren't easy,
just to let you know.
You kicked and pulled,
hit and cried.
Your tantrum reminded me
of a spoiled child.

You tried to break away
with all your might.
Yet you couldn't manage
without my light.

Deep in your soul you know
everything was done
for you to learn.
Watching your growth
delights my soul.

Now hush and listen
to my heart.
Be attentive to all my songs.

Avalanching

Watching your smile,
I paused.
Deliberately my heart
runs wild.
Ringing bells,
thundering skies,
my soul freely pirouettes
as my feet don't
touch the ground.

I reach for your hand,
I freeze.
Powerless, uninhibited,
my air with your breeze
become one.
A joyful laughter escapes
from my eyes,
avalanching on your
glittering stars.

Your moon trails
on my sun.
Our fate is clearly
a heavenly love.

Orchestrating

You and me
will never become
one body.

It doesn't matter
what the world thinks.
It doesn't matter
what the world does.

You and me
are different from
the whole.

You and me
will always
be one soul.

Keep silent…
Listen to our glow
orchestrating a blissful song,
mercifully purifying
the world's blood.

Solitude

I hear the wind
piercing my solitude.
I dare not to ask why.
Charming the moonlight
with my silence,
the pain like a wildcat
awakened my languorous soul,
alerting my sleepy white-gray cloud.

Stretching my colors
the rain stopped,
beautified my darkness.
The wind suddenly emerged
with a Milky Way and tiny stars
as they danced in my heart.
My solitude filled with
glorifying songs.

Oh Sweet, Sweet Moon!

Oh sweet, sweet moon!
Crawling in my bosom
with your sorrowful light,
your yellow cape a shield
to my night's broken wings.

Disheveled love in agony,
keeps my sleep turbulent,
my branches inarticulate sobs,
keeps a foot on my glimpse.
Unable for me to see,
to feel.

Oh sweet, sweet moon!
Don't coax me to sing.
My song will twist your light.
The night will mourn our fight.
You'll never forgive my
manifested cry.

Let me be.
Don't come to my window.
Don't tease.
Don't manipulate my heart.
Oh sweet, sweet moon!
Romancing my dreams,
you've transfigured my soul
into wind and thunder.

Aching Shadows

Bewildered I looked to hear.
I stood to see
this stirring night.
The moon unrecognized
the tearful stars,
mocking my eyes, my ears,
choking my air,
striking my patience,
soaking me with silent fear.

My body enchanted
by your single flare
as I sense your graceful arrival.
My grief twanged my spirit.
My hands maneuvered a
hopeless pain in my dusty
speechless tongue.

This night is taking
forever to sweep
the aching shadows
of your footprints
that are nailed
in my phlegmatic heart.

Dance Me with Your Soul

Come,
touch me with your eyes,
dance me with your soul.
Whisper mesmerizing words
for my heart to glow.

Don't listen
to the cosmos.
Don't pay attention
to the screams.
You and I spiritually
will always be.

Come,
hear me with your senses,
feel me with your heart.
Place your thoughts
on my bosom
as you listen to angels
singing glorious Godly songs.

Eros Dancing My Soul

Eros entered through my soul,
like fever quarreling with mind and body.
A cry of pleasure dreams
sneaking in my temple,
my heart echoing notorious
to feel your river in my eyes.

A torch set my night on fire.

Ragged clothes uncovered
my mourning begging stars,
as the moon lullaby my yearning song.

What pain is this
that has me kneeled to a prayer?
Keeping still as I watched
Eros dancing my soul
while His sword deliriously
executed my human desires.

Resurrect. A new.
My soul rejoicing life.

Throbbing Woes

You love a web
lingering inside my
gloomy dusty dream,
wakening the tempestuous night
as our silence glued
our twin echoes into mystic and sorrow.

My eyes fixated
on your twilight breeze
as your fear feared
to join my vigilant dance,
my transcendent time,
not trusting my blissful songs
wounded me with lies.

My heart avoided to believe
words that had no meaning,
but my soul listened
to your every sunbeam breath,
as my chambers filled
with silky light and anguished glow.
Restoring my throbbing woes.

Earthy Dove

A glorious spring
enhanced my moon.
With reckless songs
woke the sleepy sun.
The ground rough and sweet
flowers played hide-and-seek.
My eyes smiling to the sky.

Scenes stuffed my soul
as the four winds
ran down the hills
wrapping faith and hope,
Blessing my earthy dove
with mirth and love,
soaring in the arms of God.

Aroused

Awakened,
my soul aroused
to the wild wind,
expanding to all mankind
enlightening the blind.

I am first to admit
I am
more blind than the blind.
A glorious light sneaked
unintentionally in my
dry desert grief,
antagonizing
my child-like innocence.
Provoking my sight.

O so many visions
trembling my thoughts,
fly me to distant shores.
Engraving your name on my heart,
risking my all
so I can dance again
with your gargantuan soul.

Choose

Dreaming of
life and death,
light and darkness,
sweet and bitter,
love and hate,
happiness and grief,
joy and tears,
truth and lies,
compassion and indifference,
understanding and ignorance,
body and spirit,
heart and soul,
kindness and greed,
protecting and abusing,
awakening and dissolution,
smiling and frowning,
God and Evil.
Everything has its opposite
good and bad.
I choose good
to enlighten my growth.

She's Not!

She's not practical,
logical, reasonable.
She's not!

She's always moving out
from her comfort zone.
Her thinking is skillful.
A gift from God.
Now she knows.
There's a prophet in her,
who inspires her actions
by leading and instructing
what needs to be done.

Her faith is unbreakable.
Arrogance is not part of her.
Obedient to God.
She knows how to articulate
this and that.
She's able to see
the invisible.
She's been labeled an odd,
a nerd.
But what many do not know
is that she works for the Lord.

Weeping

My sad heart,
my teary eyes,
sitting silently
in front of the moonlight.
No stars tonight,
no milky way,
no galaxies
to take me away.
My soul is charmless,
weeping with the sighing wind,
waiting for the day light
to fly free.
Darkness has me
beneath her feet.
Searching for light
so I can see.

Restless Soul

I travel
by air, by wind, by foot,
claiming your air, your breath,
the wind touching your face,
the earth holding your balance.

Passing morning, evening, night
the sun speaks to me
of your freight,
the evening mist warns me
of your weary eyes,
the night approaches me
with naked moon
revealing your silent pain,
your anguish grief.

I travel
non-stop with my restless soul
untouched by fear,
extinguishing your rusty thunder
as I set your eyes free.

Your Moon

Watching your sunset,
your face rejuvenate
my delightful soul,
refusing to be apart
from your hot-icy touch,
striving to feed you love.

Your whistling clouds
forbidden my dance,
your moon crippled my stars
turning this night without wings
melting darkness wrapped
around my arms and feet.

Your words are losing
their flavor in my heart,
numbness and skepticism
taken over my unrestricted love.
Your foggy vision entertained
my golden-silver whirring dream.

Scattered thoughts
praying on its knees
for this dazzling pain
to be drowned in
midnight's thunder,
lightening, scream.

Loitering

I shall wait and see,
eyeing for your
silence, your quiet walk,
your blossoming songs,
to take hold of my piercing wind,
igniting a flame between
your gaze and my
painful maze.

Loitering without a clock,
courageously
I shall wait and see,
if your prairie flowers
will dress my soul
with your summer wild sun,
kissing my wilderness
with your rainfall breeze.

I shall wait and see.
Not rushing time,
ruffling my tongue to speak.
Only the promise
we need to keep.

The Chambers of My Heart

My vision surfed upon
your rebellious sea,
catching your waves
embroidering hymns,
towered a twilight
in my soul.
Dancing to your violin,
a joyful pain glittered
enchanting fireworks in my being.

Out of breath
inverted your shore,
my eyes with your eyes
touched heaven on earth.
Mysterious you caught in my dream.
The ocean whistled, winked,
waking a forgotten dream.

Taunted by the wind,
my rain drenched your
slothful walk.
In the chambers of my heart
I hear you roar.

Instrument of Love

I look into your eyes
and saw your broken heart.
I reached out and gave you
my instrument of Love.
Your alignment
Glorifies God.

My Crucifixion

It was easier to
give you my body
instead I gave you my soul.
Loving you has been
my crucifixion,
my resurrection.
I was transformed.
The Spirit of God
resides in my blood.

Searching

Navigating the smudged lonely night
as I search among the flickering stars,
the half-moon wavering rushed to uncover
your playful face hidden
in the wind and rain.

Don't run away!
Can you not see?
Your sky keeps me up
burdening my grieving soul
since you abandoned our dance and song.

Fearful unable to
see me in the eyes,
you jumped, ran,
from cloud to cloud,
not knowing what to do next,
a sigh took over my speech
surrendering to hide-and-seek.

Oh! My sweet, sweet desire
don't tease my solitude
with your dark dreamy eyes.

Shielding Your Anger

My heart vibrates
as I walk through
your meadow of silence.
With a broken smile
your river runs
through my lost moonlight.

Aching for your eyes
to penetrate my wearisome soul,
your echo mocking my waterfall.
Alone, admitting to your thorns.

Oh! The pain like a disease
crawled in my eyes.
Blinded me.

Hearing your crying
disturbed my peace.
Outstretched my body and arms,
shielding your anger
with my eternal love.

Nature's Cacophony

O God can you hear
my plea?
Bewildered, standing alone,
not knowing which way to go.

I don't recognize
the sun and the moon.
Nature's cacophony
blocks my gentle breeze,
hiding my gratifying dream.

A storm comes my way
each time I give,
crushes my blind heart
that refuses to see.

I stand alone.
I turn the other cheek.
Humility takes my hand
enlightening my peaceful soul.

Dangerous Love

Regaining my energy
as your smile abducted
my heart's sleepy butterfly.

Your smooth eyes crawled
inside my divinity,
awakening shadows,
stirring my crumbled dreams.

Listening to your tip-toe,
my silence wept
as it tumbled inside
your shining blaze.

Dangerous love
touched my soul.
Afraid to fly again,
the pain a river of tears
mesmerizing my trance.

I've been waiting for eternity
to unite with your songs.
Do you not know?
Your soul with my soul
echoes the same tone.

I Dare

I dare not
to look in your eyes,
your sorrow drips pain
in my twilight gaze.
No matter where I see
your eyes tend
to follow me.

Your fear battled
with my unstained love
as our souls in bliss
merged as one.
Your echo woken
my heavenly star.

Whispering not to disturb
your aphotic weeping,
gracefully without a sound
I mended your wounded heart
with my burning candle-light.

I dare
to look in your eyes.

Love Enduring All

Wild witty grief
languished in my soul,
stealing the light from my eyes,
wounding tearfully my sight.

Love enduring all.

Fear and hope perished.
The heart dressed in black,
no song to sing,
no dance to dance.
Forgetful of the cause,
surrendering to a dying dream.

Love enduring all.

Mournful my every step,
lamenting my seasons.
Lying upon the broken moon,
ignominy stroke my woeful face.
Stars and wind
dwelling in my extinguished flame.

Love enduring all.

Like A Gypsy

Tell me,
why is your silence
shouting at me?
Why is your loneliness
wrapping wisdom
around my ancient brave feet?

Why do I see and hear
your morning dew?
Your night a frameless moon,
your fighting stars
a blaze upon my heart.
Listening to your crying
disrupts my polished song.
Like a gypsy I chase
to find your sun.

Tell me,
or maybe you should not.
Your silence
is my cross, my miracle.
How do I know?
My witness is my Lord.

Solo Dance

I must confess…
I love no other
as I love your exuberant
smile and eyes.
Smooth is your voice
upon my tears,
gives my heart a solo dance.

Our eyes touched.
I kissed your hand,
your storm subsided
inside my dreamy land.

Pondering Thoughts

Inhaling darkness,
my body feels the space
between the moon's shadow
and the flickering stars.
Oblivion of my broken heart
my journey endless
with many curves,
it takes me to crushed Winters,
wilted Springs,
shady Summers,
broken Autumns.

Searching careless,
keeping empty hopes,
the night is without applause.
My body plundered,
abandoned my soul.
Exhaling wrecked winds,
chasing clouds
from my pondering thoughts.

Rainbow to My Storm

All that I really love
is You.
You're quench to my thirst,
spark to my flame,
rhythm to my pathos,
light to my melancholia.

You're all
that I really love.

You're my tranquility to my ocean,
rainbow to my storm,
sun to my rain,
wings to my broken flutter.

You're all
that I really love.

You're my Spring to my Autumn,
Summer to my Winter,
wildflowers to my expired dreams,
stability to my wobbling hope.

You're all
that I really love.

You're my songs to my solitude,
dance to my soul,

exuberant voice to my silence,
path to my mystical walk.

You're my alpha, my omega.
You're my Spiritual home.

Fleeting Dust

Reaching out,
catching your dust,
my eyes halted
in your angelic wind.
Standing silent, alone,
watching your springtime
congregate with my Winter's whisper,
my Summer's breeze,
remaining enthusiastic
as I observed
your morning glow.
Your dust unexpectedly
mesmerized my bruised soul.
Hunting your jasmine
with my disarmed love,
the aroma melted my scattered heart.
Kneeling I kissed
your fleeting dust.

Divine Silence

Feeling your pain
as if my own,
unable to control
the outcome.
Not knowing a thing,
with a heart
full of tears and sorrow,
uninhabited watching your darkness
unfolding into my light.

Your soul with my soul
sustaining a wounded promise,
frightened by an unknown
divine silence.
Tangling your moon
with my sun,
your storm with my rainbow,
exhausting the undying dream.

Feeling your pain,
my sky intertwined
with your hidden tenderness.
A new born song flourished,
embracing fearless
our fragmented tango.

Your Alluring Smile

Unfulfilled desires
keep me up at nights.
My soul on fire,
travels your darkness,
merging with your destiny.
My senses, shadows,
washing out your woes,
striking out crawling words.

Underneath the newborn moon
my eyes wondered in silence
as tears grieved the empty space,
the dance without steps,
the songs without lyrics,
the music without rhythm,
roads without destination,
grieving ferociously.

Caught in the four seasons,
bleeding,
the stars sowing your eyes
inside my solitary heart
as loneliness endured
your alluring smile
playfully teasing my
drenching dream.

Take My Hand

Do not wander aimlessly
away from me.
You'll be lost.
How will I find you?
Your landmarks defeated
by dust and rain.
My eyes unable to hear
your movements,
my ears unable to catch
your night's falling star.
Take my hand,
hold my heart,
climb my soul.
Do not interrupt our walk.
Do not wander aimlessly
away from me.
Stay still. Listen.
Together fearless
our journey will
take us home.

Wrecking My Anchor

Shameless I reached out,
touched your eyes with my eyes.
Your pain a volcano,
nested your hot lava in my heart,
erupting my tranquility.

Covered with tears and thorns,
your darkness hanging loose,
acquainted with my light.
Your crying whistled to my joy.

Your grief wind-storm
nailed my purity to your cross,
wrecking my anchor
as I was surrounded by
your aching words.

Thirsty to kiss
your eyes again with my eyes
regardless of your whining.
My soul danced your soul
as your lava orchestrated our steps.

A Foolish Poet

Day and night
like a foolish poet
trying to unlock your soul
without a key,
only using love.
I called your cloudy sky
to meet with my bright night.

Falling like a feather
on your feet,
you crushed drop by drop
the life out of me.
A nightingale cried,
lamenting the betrayed dream.

The poet without wings
recreated eternal love
protecting your insensible heart.

I Walk Alone

I do not need an audience,
or someone's approval.
I do not need to be liked.
My path is carved
with thunder and lightning.
My face against the winds,
my body wrapped in rains,
my mind full of ecstasy.
I walk alone
having God as my strength,
Jesus as my guide.

I do not need much.
I just need the sun on my face,
the moon as my friend,
oceans to play with my soul,
mountains to carry my goals,
darkness to sooth my light.
And you, you my dream
to fight my plight.

Nailed on a Cross

Sweet is your madness
without a reason,
without a cause,
has me nailed on a cross.

Wondered what
you'll do next,
shielded my soul
from your bitterness
and angry words.

I stepped way
with bleeding heart,
my body unable
to hold me up.

You pouted and screamed,
blocking windows,
breaking doors,
you sold me
to cover all your wrongs.

May God have mercy
on your exasperated soul.

My Love

Be silent my love,
listen closely
to the praising wind,
the giggling rain.
Watch the moonlight
dimming her eyes,
the stars embracing
the glory of night.

Be silent my love,
feel the clouds,
smell the flowers,
use the air to delight
your frown with a smile.
Let your busy dreams
entertain our untamed dance.

Be silent my love,
taste nature's bliss.
The earth sings our songs.
Oh weep from joy
as our tears restore
our promise once was made.

To love so deep
my love,
causes pain.

Your Shadow Follows Me

I take your shadow with me.
It follows me
everywhere I go.
Breathless,
your eyes glowing
in my dawn.

The color of your love
intertwines with my
turbulent sea,
yearning for your whispers.

Unknown to me
where you begin and
where I end.
My heart bruised by
your golden wind.

Impossible to be alone,
your shadow always follows me.
Years have walked by
yet your voice captures
my senses.

Memories raise
me to the sky.
I take your shadow with me.
Until I die.

Looking

I am looking.
Can you not tell?
Why do you ask
what am I looking for?
Is it out of curiosity?
Or do you really care?
Please do not lie,
do not confuse,
do not be another Pinocchio.
I'm looking
into your soul
to touch your treasures.

Assassinating My Pain

I stare at the moon,
patiently waiting
as the stars prune my appetite.

An owl keeps me company,
reciting poetry
while my eyes fixated
on the nights' fragrance.

Your gardenias, carnations,
orchids, lilacs, jasmines
arrived joyfully
assassinating my pain.

Love executed doubts
as the moon unloaded
your presence
inside my empty embrace.

Ripples of Joy and Tears

I sat under a willow tree,
watching the whispering butterflies
gathering sprinkled sunlight,
as my eyes spilled
waves of kisses,
mischievously
writing your name across
the blue crystal sky
for the world to see.

Ripples of joy and tears
tender and gentle
submitting my forever love
for the approval of God.
Angels faithfully applaud
the union of our souls.
You and I eagerly refused to die.

The grass, the flowers, the pond
shimmering silently in the moonlight
as I craved to touch your eyes.
My trembling breath
careless awaked our
forgotten dance.

Clouded Heart and Soul

Intimate with my silence,
liberating my agony
with loving thoughts of you.
My clouded heart and soul
peacefully subsided
as God molded my painful song
into a song of a new
purified horizon.

An invisible breeze
caressed my unassisted grief
that for years was hidden inside
my dry tears.

Your absence softly guided
my lonely orphan
to your sun and rain,
nourishing my hunger
with humility and love,
slowly inheriting light and peace.
I am wounded
no more.

The Poetry of Your Soul

Sleepless, powerless,
yearning for your eyes.
Your speechless words,
the lyrics from my mind
have me prophesying
the poetry of your soul,
the wilderness of your heart.
Unwilling to give you up.

Looking at the mellow sky,
delighted by the tearful moon,
the dwelling broken stars,
cherishing your smile
while lighting my melancholy night.

Sleepless, restless,
vigilant is my dream,
searches to touch
your lavishing smile.
I stumbled against
your sky and your Milky Way.

Harmonizing darkness
with your choral song
your absence disappeared
alleviating pain from my heart.
Your whispers lullabied my sleep
to sleep.

Pain and Love

Your fear nailed my heart.
Poetry came out of my soul,
uniting pain and love.

Obedient

It's never been my way.
It's always been God's way.
When I walk away
from His path
His hand takes me
back where He wants me to be.
My Free Will always
being tested.
His way is the only
way I know.
Obedient
to all His calls.

To Be

I want to be
your air
and your light.

The Hunger of My Soul

Invisible is my God.
His glance penetrates
the hunger of my soul.
My aching heart
digs for His lonely star
to heal my wounded spirit.

I'm not amongst the herd.
My solitary walk
is filled with abundance.
His compassion and tenderness
fulfills my dance and prayer.

My God blossoms
in my dust and light.
His touch cultivates
my infinite vision and knowledge.
His extraordinary hands
lift me from my knees.
I stand in the desire
of His fire.

No Gender

I have no gender.
I am neither masculine
nor feminine.
Limited are my needs.
My human form
is the chamber of my soul.
I have been kissed by God.
My world turned
inside-out.
A fearless love fueled
my every
action and desire.

Boring

Life without you
is boring.
You're the only one
who can stir my soul
with magic.

The Power of Love

Uncontrolled by limits,
in the rain, in the sunshine
dancing with God.
He's the only one.
Not a day goes by
without conversing with Him,
whispering in His ear,
trusting Him with my heart.

Obedient,
serving His word.
Overpowered by His light,
faithfully I walk His walk.
My soul, my life,
devoted to His talk.

Letting go of
man-made rules,
this and that,
the maybe and the not,
the why and the how,
the could and the should
that imprison my thoughts.

I only listen to the
rules of my Lord.
After all it's all about
the power of love.
Don't you know?

Your Colors and Aromas

Your soul congregated with my soul
in this Spring God-like morning.
Something pink, red, white,
purple, yellow,
brought your wind in my fated sun,
perking my slender air.
Suddenly longing to caress
our forgotten dance.

In front of flowers, bees, trees,
mountains, oceans, skies,
my heart transfixed on your eyes,
as my feet tangled with your
pain and joy.

Blind, aphonie, motionless,
breathing your colors and aromas,
taking your hand in my hand,
engaging your smile
with my tender song,
realizing no storm, no thunder
can destroy our adventurous
daring hearts.

Chasing Wants

You want me to be
your love story.
I want you to be
my whispers.

You want passion,
adventure, newness.
I want your eyes,
your heart, your soul.

You want…
I want…
Chasing wants!

Let's combined
your love story
with my whispers.

Now watch…
Eyes, heart, soul,
renewing
passion in adventure.
Fireworks.

Miracle of Love

I crawled out of your chaos,
unrolled out of your pain.
Silenced my screams,
froze my logic,
killed my desires.
Walked away
from your agony.
Emptied my soul
from your fire.
Only so you can feel
the miracle of love.

Flames

My spirit
paced back and forth,
as your voice echoed
in my dark forest.

Loose clouds,
emotional winds,
stormy rains
captivated your soul,
casting it
in my silence,
flaming my unvoiced song.

Unnoticed
my wounded heart
cultivated tears and pain.
My sky lit in flames.
And you my love,
You
subsided in my veins.

No Need

My thoughts are made
of you,
seducing my walk, my smile.
There's no space
for the sun, the moon,
the falling stars.
I am all taken.
By you.

Your waves of love
mesmerizing my whispers.
My air dances to your
glorious darkness and light.
Your rain and dust
cleans out my sight.

No need for me
looking back.
No need for me
looking ahead.
No matter where,
no matter what,
you're my universe,
you're my God.

Poetry in My Soul

It was summertime
when I was introduced
to your eyes and smile.
Your dawn waved in despair,
provoking my sleepy pathos.
Aggravated,
my sorrowful moon was teased
by your playful sun.

I beg for you to stop
but your rhymes
rattled poetry in my soul,
binding your breeze
with my whispers.

My solitude dressed
with your noble spirit.
Your colorful pedals formed
a river for my delight.
Your sky, sun, birds,
flowers, butterflies, trees
gathered love and light.

I must confess…
I've never before
lost the way I'm lost
inside your soul.
Uniting joy and pain.

Dazzling Whistles

Hissing rain
I can hear your
whirring passing through
my nakedness,
mocking my clouded eyes.

You become one
with my winter's rhythm,
as you flood
my spring with flowers,
leaving me hungry
for your dazzling whistles.

Dear Pain

O my dear
inseparable pain,
you come in my
solitary loneliness
to dress me with words,
to dance my silence
with your flames,
to burn me until I am ashes.

What you
do not know dear pain,
is that the pain you cause me
keeps me in tune,
connects me deeper
with the Lord,
gives light to my soul,
makes my heart dive
inside the unknown,
spits me out wiser and strong.

An Archipelago throbs
in my unveiled love.
Dear pain.
Now go away.
Your job is done.

No Room for Fear

Fear and Love
can't coexist.

Fear absorbs darkness.
Love absorbs light.

Fear dances with pain.
Love dances with joy.

Fear cripples the heart.
Love enhances the soul.

Fear threatens health.
Love heals wounds.

Fear creates evil.
Love creates goodness.

Fear fuels jealousy.
Love embraces trust.

Fear builds arrogance.
Love spreads gratefulness.

Fear complicates.
Love simplifies.

Fear stifles.
Love clarifies.

There's no room for fear
where there's Love.

Rejecting Love

You may taunt me.
Your insulting remarks
tell me what you
carry in your heart.

You may place all
the blame on me,
accusing me out of fear,
yet deep in your soul
the truth dwells.

Loving you
was my crucifixion
and also my resurrection.
Your blindness has made you
unable to see.
Rejecting love,
you have pulled me apart,
mistrusting my gentle touch.

I love no one
more than I love you.
And if you don't believe me
ask the Lord
who has listened
to my prayers all along.

Your Touch on My Soul

No need to be liked.
No need to be accepted.
No need to fit in.
No need to be understood.
No need for approval.
No need for the throne.

A need for solitude
so I can feel
your touch on my soul.

Surrendered

I gazed in your eyes.
Standing still, powerless,
your glance penetrated
my vulnerability.

You undressed my midnight mist,
forming a prismatic union
between my soul and your soul.
Your fragrance mesmerized
my clear fate.
Half sleeping,
your voice inspired
a blue dream
that has me sailing
on a glowing moon,
pampering
my airy desires.

I gazed in your eyes,
my heart caught on red flames
as I surrendered to you luscious fire.

Your Aromatic Jungle

I've searched for you
in every fairy tale,
in every poem,
in every whisper,
in every daylight,
in every lighthouse,
in every journey.

I've searched for you.

I've search for you
in every tear,
in every joy,
in every breath,
in every space,
in every storm,
in every rainbow.

I've searched for you.

An emanated dream
pulled me in your aromatic jungle.

Kneeled to a Prayer

Emulating God,
His love and light
walks me through His paradise.
My daily conversations
undictated, unrehearsed,
speaks with Him
in a humbled tongue.
He listens attentively
while guiding my every
thought and action,
purifying my wounded heart.
His presence transforms
my pain into a harmonious dance.
His arms energized
my body, mind, and soul.
Connected to Him
my spirit radiates His peace.
An outcry of joy
has me kneeled to a prayer.

Soul Drenched in Faith

With a naked eye
I embraced your fear,
claiming your distorted
pain as if my own.

Your lonely cry like a bell
climbed my ears
causing a divine rapture.
Without a doubt
my soul drenched in Faith
pulling your dark veil
from your deep dark eyes
enchasing your light.

Intimate with your silence,
I reached out and touched
your grief,
perpetuating my testimonial
of your gifted soul.
My selfless love
engulfed
in your lavishing spirit.

Wild Outcry

I looked around,
you're nowhere to be found.
I asked the trees, the birds, the bumblebees,
the grasshoppers, the frogs, the flowers,
the suns, the rivers, the skies, the clouds,
the animals, the moons, the stars,
if they have seen you.
They all exclaimed a powerful No!

I wondered where to walk,
where else to search.
Do I need to scream your name
for the universe to hear my plea?
I no longer could find my path.
Little more, or little less
my wild outcry
dropped in God's ears.

Suddenly you appeared,
dressed with summer's breeze,
only so you can ease
my exhausted fears.

Weeping from Joy

Your stars tickled
my senses,
while your celestial wisdom
touched my divinity.
Unassuming I gazed
at your glorious night
wishing for your Milky-Way
to dance with my starving vigilance.

Contemplating,
my silence eavesdropping
on your half-moon,
listening to your whispers,
mysteriously caressing
my wounds.

Faithful to your wild soul,
to your misty glow.
Weeping from joy
as you gently
kissed my soul.

Your Maze

I ran my fingers
through your soul,
obsessing to heal
your dark pain with my light.

Wearing raggedy clothes,
I disguised my spirit
with my human form
so you wouldn't be afraid
as my air touched
your dreamy eyes.

Patiently waited
to witness your
shapeless echoes,
barking to escape.
Forming a pathway,
I scanned your waves
in a harmonious dance.

Free at last from your maze.

White Magnolias

Catching the sunlight
to fill my empty dream
that once was
making love with
your mysterious eyes.

My dawn no longer
searches for your wildflowers.
No longer matters if
you love me, love me not.

My crippled heart
with broken roads
naked and dry.
Empty from all desires.
Your moonlight
no longer gives me light.

My white magnolias bloomed
as you set
my soul on fire.

Mesmerizing Echoes

Many years have gone by
without a knock.
My door was left unlocked.
I waited
day after day,
year after year,
but your sunbeam
never approached my door.

Your wind
came and went.
Leaving behind
mesmerizing echoes
to tease my unfulfilled dream.
Still waiting
and hoping
to be touched
by your poetic soul.

I must not complain
if I want to hear
your coming storm.

His Fiery Sword

I speak to God
about you.
He smiles.
I pray to God
about you.
He listens.

I wait.
He waits.

I look closer,
He steps away.

I question, why?
He answers, why not?

I turn my image into dust.
He turns me into Love.

I touch His face.
He turns Himself to you.

Now I know
how much I
love the Lord.

You and I connected by
His fiery sword.

Love was at Stake

Drop by drop
I collected your grey grief,
feeling your rigorous pain
going through my heart and spirit.

Deaf and blind
not paying attention,
I climbed down, picked you up,
carried your cross as if my own,
to enlighten your broken soul.

Manifested signs of love,
your weight emerged
scraping our
trials and tribulations
before God.

It wasn't a cheap price to pay
when Love was at stake.

To Death Do Us Part

I caught you
staring at my joyful soul.
The more you stared,
the more I danced.
Entertaining angels
congregating
in your wild wind,
kissing my smooth dew,
tangling your song
with my gentle echoes.

Love is created
for two,
not for one or three.
Staring at my solitude
a garden grew in
your heart and soul,
melting away your anger,
your hurt and harmful air.

Staring back at you,
you ran away,
fearing to be caught,
not realizing that
your soul with my soul
are one.
Inseparable
till death do us part.

Your Glorious Light

Unfit to touch your soul.
Sleepless,
my heart thirsty
for your desert.
Watching the yellow moon
agonizing over
your scattered stars,
my eyes searching
for your stagnated garden.

Your breeze like
the sound of a flute
trailing through
my vigilant dream,
keeps me restless as I
wait to hear
your golden-silver wings.

If not tonight
then when?
When can I expect
your arrival?
Like fever you ran
through my heart
as I wait
for the morning dew
to spank the night
so I can feel your
glorious light.

Your Enormous Sky

I want to touch
your air
with my rain.
To smell
your wildflowers
with my six senses.
To dive
like a fool
in your flower garden
and dress you
with my love.

I want to feel
your storm
with my rainbow.
To see
your naked heart
with my shadow.
To lose my soul
in your enormous sky.
To sing to your
colorful paradise.
And free me
in your wild wind.

Our Eyes Intermingled

I crumbled an orchid into dust
to harmonize your tears
with my pain.
Fixing my gaze
upon your holy breeze
as your prophet blossomed
enthusiasm in
my screaming wind.

Your wildflower soul
danced with my gypsy river
mixing Spring and Fall.
My Winter melted
in your Summer
as our eyes intermingled.

Locking my throbbing heart
to your poetic silent touch.
My soul collided with your
victorious thrilling songs.

Lashing Out

Storms. Thunders.
A hurricane in your eyes
sparked lighting
in my disturbed sleep.
Unable to rest,
your hunted wind
keeps me on my toes.
Breaking into silence
as you bang unexpectedly
on my soul.

Lashing out,
your transparent scream
squeezed my heart
as I am longing
for your blue-white sky
and your sunshine touch.
How can I settle
in your gloomy wilderness?
You have me dwelling
in your obliviousness.

Don't Be Afraid of Death

Don't be afraid of death.
Your soul glitters to escape
from your weeping
roaming grief.
I'll be waiting
on the other side
to hold you with my breeze,
to caress you with my eyes.

Don't be afraid of death.
Your heart dances in my light.
Watch. Stay still.
My undying love
will carry you
to My blissful sky.
It's always
you and I.

Don't be afraid of death.
You'll never be forgotten.
My dust will
orchestrate our songs.
All will be perfect
as you will finally
be waltzing in My arms.

My Innocent Sea Breeze

Forgive me
for I do not know
how to love you less.

My love an ocean,
unintelligible my waves
genuine reach for your
poetic soul
to connect
my innocent sea breeze
with your sailing
stumbling song.

Oh! How
I admire your
abandoned moon,
your soft whispers
blurring
crazy desires.
Untamable is your light.

Forgive me
for my madness
that tumbles
at your sight.

I'm Possessed

Shamelessly,
my heart talked
about love.

But no one listened.
Not even you.

You turned your back.
The dream fainted
inside my eyelashes.

Empty.
Alone.
A new dream
appeared on the horizon.

Unbelievable how
I'm possessed.
Without love
all dreams are dead.

Touched by His Light

Forbidden fears
have pushed my doubts aside,
allowing the Lord
to show me Faith and Heaven.

An endless road
took me near and far,
low and high.
Through passing storms
my soul thrived.
Renewing darkness
as I was touched by
His light.

There are no excuses,
laziness, drama, blaming,
repetition of lack of trust
which stifle a promised heart.

I walked away,
left all alone,
holding on to pain
mercifully calling
on my Lord.

Resurrected
my Body, Mind and Soul.

Feeling your Agony

How many centuries
have I counted
your tears upon
my aching heart?

Morning and night
my thoughts trimmed
your moonlight rain,
sending chills
to my lonely dusk.

You're making
all the noise,
disturbing my sleepy stars.
My eyes searching
in your dense fog,
feeling your agony
with my many scars.

Motionless your
shadow loitering
in my rippled breeze.
Your noise has me
traveling on your
wild seas.

The Gift from God

The soul is selective.
It will rather be alone
than to be caught
in lies, chaos,
ill-conceived thoughts.

A turmoiled heart
needs a place to be quiet,
away from words, actions,
to stay still even when
fire erupts,
burning dreams and
hidden seeds.

The body needs to stretch,
breathe, walk, run,
to be kissed by the sun.
To step away from conditions
that would leave
deep scars.

Oh! The spirit
the gift from God,
can't be suffocated
by shame and guilt.
Freedom
is what it seeks.

Without Agenda

She's small,
without agenda.
Lost in the wind,
like a feather,
tumbling in the air,
trusting a butterfly
to raise her to the sky.

No, she does not
want to reach the sun.
She does not
want to be
one with the stars.
She's just a feather.

She does not walk
on earth.
Humans tend
to step on her.
She moves out of the way.
She loves being a feather.
Transparent.

You Come and Go

The evening sat quietly
by my window.
The sky blushed
as the moon cha-cha danced
the stars.
Intoxicated, the night
redeemed its virtues,
as the Milky-Way
tamed my dawn.

Hungry and thirsty,
recklessly I watched
for your image to appear.
My eyes filled
with grey-white clouds,
weeping, accumulating
anticipation to hear
your night's golden song.

Lonely, yet not alone,
your eyes confusing
my restless soul
as you come and go,
letting me know.
In darkness your light
sparks my heart to glow.

Weepy Heart

Deep within my soul
spring flowers bloomed
and so did hope.

I called upon my Lord,
wishing on the falling star,
for secrets to be kissed
by His auriferous Sun.

My every step thrived
with a magic wand
to regain the flames
of my dying mourning love.

A midnight cry
imprisoned my weepy heart.
Starving desires
flourished as I yearned
for your gentle touch.

Your silver splendor dust
caressed my
lamenting tears,
delighting my
sluggish fears.

Flying

The knife
on my back
didn't go wasted.

Poetry spilled
out of my soul.

Can you not see?
Colorful turned my wings.
I'm flying free.

.

Talk to Me

Talk to me
not with words.
Talk to me
with your eyes.

Keep silent
so I can hear
your gifted joy,
so I can feel
your shattered grief,
so I can touch
your agonized smile.

Talk to me
not with words.
Talk to me
with your pain.

Keep still
so I can feel
your roaring love,
so I can taste
your broken heart.

Embrace Your Truth

I remain obscured.
Don't come close,
don't walk away.
You do not know,
so how can you be sure
if not knowing
your thoughts are true?

You think you know,
but your views
are self-served.
Manipulating light
pretending to open your mind
to what is
and what is not.
Then how can you say
you truly love?

How can you
give me
the purity of your heart,
when your heart
is tangled in a wild storm,
not letting me come
closer to your soul.

Each time I approach
your vicious lightening
stops me on my tracks,
fearing your tiger

who lives in your
distant glance.

I remain obscured
only to allow you
to embrace your truth.

Exchange of Our Glances

My heart melts
every time
I feel you in my air.

Like a thousand candles,
dripping hot sweat
wrinkling my dream,
isolating my view,
belonging only
to your fire storm.

My soul in your silence
listens to your
shy desires
as your fear
dances with my shadow,
extinguishing our blaze.

There isn't a
cupid with bow and arrow,
only the exchange
of our glances
which intertwined
your heart with my heartbeat.
Creating a thunder.

I love You

I don't need to
tell you
I love you,
they're just plain words.

I proved it
with my actions
through my bleeding soul.

Breaking My Silence

You hover my thoughts
with your cluttered poetic prayer.
God listened then He turned to me.
His light showed me the way.

Your dancing giggled
my silent cloudy Spring,
as my Angel bruised
by your dazzling daylight.
Yearning to touch your eyes,
my hands sky blue,
painted your shadow
in my foehn wind
and gusty rain.

O my willing heart
hassled with your Holy
grievous lonely song,
breaking my silence
with your night's
mocking star.

I praised your sunset
as you humbled your kiss
on my dawn.

You Are

You're my rose, my thorn,
my Spring, my Winter,
you're my painful light,
my joyful darkness.

You're my tears, my smile,
my weird wind, my delightful sin.
You're my bravest touch,
my glorious blissful love.

You're my mournful standing song,
my heavenly whisper tagging rhythm.
You're my stable heartbeat,
my bleeding crown dream.

You're everything and my nothing,
my magical white and blue.
You're my breath in every morning,
my fog in my strange twilight.

You're my beast, my butterfly,
my speechless caress,
my weeping moonlight.
You're my everlasting Life.

Scattered Thoughts

I took my broken heart
and turned it into poetry.

~~~ * ~~~

Vision is having the ability
to see the invisible.

~~~ * ~~~

Once you're touched by God you can never go back.

~~~ * ~~~

It's what we choose to see ...
Observation needs stillness and quietness.
To be silent is to have an insight to all God's gifts...

~~~ * ~~~

Be the sky not the weather.
Have no limits to your dreams.
Don't be afraid to fly.

~~~ * ~~~

Close your eyes and feel your heart.
Allow yourself to hear your music.
Dance to you own rhythm regardless who's watching.

~~~ * ~~~

Thinking is the language of the Soul.

~~~* ~~~

It's my enduring Faith and Hunger
that turn lights on... It's about selflessness.

~~~*~~~

Your every insult strengthens the love I have for you.
I turn the other cheek.

~~~*~~~

Don't be concerned about falling...
focus on rising after the fall.

~~~*~~~

Life is about moving, creating, loving, dreaming,
and having Faith in God's Plan.

~~~*~~~

Simplicity is the harmony of the soul.

~~~*~~~

It takes a little fog for one to see clearly...

Nightingale

The nightingale came
full of charisma,
wakening my drowsy dream,
singing a love song
for my wilted heart to hear.

The night weeping,
the moon colorless
in her silky dress,
the stars naked stopped
radiating light,
as darkness murdered
my innocent child-like soul.

Closing my eyelids,
as I listened
to the nightingale's song,
his wings running up and down,
in and out,
begging for me not to quit,
trying to subside
your cruel winds
that have me
caught in your hurricanes
unable to see.

The nightingale's song
became my only hope,
my only love.

Interconnected

I did uncover
my soul.
You were too blind
to see.
You were focusing
how to hide
your soul,
so I wouldn't see.

Do you think
I did not know?

Haven't you
realized?
What does it take?
Let go!
See.

We're related
since centuries ago.
Your soul with my soul
interconnected
in divinity.

Don't you know?

Undying Love

I found your laughter
among my shapeless glow,
your eyes gazing
at my airy breeze,
waiting for your sky
to touch my gloomy dream.

My darkness suddenly disappeared.

I heard your playful song
pirouetting in my solitary heart,
your delicate reserved touch
like a rainbow colored
my uninspired soul,
giving my blizzard dust
the foundation of your undying love.

My silence overflowed
with your ocean foamy waves
cleansing me from tears and pain.
Your voice a wizard,
tickled my moon and stars.
I was kissed by your softly windy nymph.
Under your spell
I felt your igniting spark
dancing on my Holy Ark.

Eternal Dawn

The rain came down,
softly wiped my tears,
gently bent down and kissed
my trembling fears.

With open arms caressed
my face with
her pearl raindrops,
whispering this and that,
changing my heart of hearts.

My tears subsided,
a smile took over
my frowning lips,
my face without a doubt
found my exuberant
eternal dawn
loving your gasping star.

Hoping

Walking from cloud to cloud
my vision limited by your mist,
my heart seeing your blazing soul
trespassing my dotted planets,
brutalizing my lonely storm.

Reaching out,
floating on thick air,
catching your glance with my breath,
hoping to dance
one last dance.
Your eyes with my eyes
flamed the sky red.

The night dropped her black veil,
turning the stars into a chandelier,
the rusted moon
intimately whispered,
harmonizing our aching brittle song
as we slowly pulled apart.

Only to dance
to a new Heavenly song.

I've Lost You

I've lost you,
only to find you
deeper in my dreams,
playful in my heart,
colorful dust in my eyes,
love whispers in my ears,
sensation in my touch,
tenderness in my feelings,
sweetness in my tongue.

I've lost you,
only to find you hidden
a gentle God in my soul.

Your Voice

Your voice,
O your voice,
tumbled in my naked heart,
provoked a gracious rhythm,
kissed my tearful star.

Alone,
drenched
in midnight's lonely dew,
your eyes united
with my wild gypsy soul.

Your voice,
O your voice,
a lullaby
in my thirsty ears,
mesmerized my lonely song,
caressed my yearning wind.

In my solitude is where
you come alive,
where I can feel your touch.
In my solitude is where
your voice fills me
with your enormous love.

Your voice,
O your voice,
soothed my turbulent sea,
gracefully sailing
in harmonious bliss.

Encountered God

I see your beauty
with the purity of my soul,
my eyes touch
your clinging breeze.
Your laughter congregates
with my solitary star.
The sky mystified
by your supreme dance,
allowed white clouds
to carve your distractive path.

Without a body,
without an earth,
cleansing fears
purifies your shouting grief
not letting go
of joyful tears.

I see your glitters
forming love
that has me captured
in your magical lantern.
I encountered God.

My God, Eros of Love

My God, Eros of Love,
obscured in your mysticism.
Your aphorism upon my soul
gives unity, light
upon my broken walk.

You fill my solitude
with your alphas and omegas.
Your stormy skies
calms my euphoric heart
as Your touch
brightens my lamenting song.

My God, Eros of Love,
You have twisted me
in various forms,
my colors transparent
for Your heaven to view.

Fearless, tumultuous,
You come to me.
My aching pain,
my wounded rest,
courageously plows my
darkness so I can see.

My God, Eros of Love,
You magnify my vision.
Inside Your palm
my spirit glows.
Only to You I give
my Mind, Body and Soul.

Made in the USA
Middletown, DE
16 March 2022

62773067R00080